MAR 2008

What Do You Know About
The Civil War

PowerKiDS
press
New York

Lynn George

Published in 2008 by The Rosen Publishing Group, Inc.
29 East 21st Street, New York, NY 10010

First Edition

Editor: Joanne Randolph
Book Design: Kate Laczynski
Photo Researcher: Nicole Pristash

Photo Credits: Cover, pp. 1, 7, 8, 9, 10, 12, 13, 14, 15, 16, 17, 18, 19, 20, 21 © Getty Images; pp. 5, 11 Shutterstock.com.

Library of Congress Cataloging-in-Publication Data

George, Lynn.
  What do you know about the Civil War? / Lynn George. — 1st ed.
      p. cm. — (20 questions : History)
  Includes index.
  ISBN 978-1-4042-4187-9 (library binding)
  1. United States—History—Civil War, 1861–1865—Miscellanea—Juvenile literature. 2. Children's questions and answers. I. Title.
  E468.9.G46 2008
  973.7—dc22

                                        2007029518

Manufactured in the United States of America

Contents

The Civil War 4

1. Who said your way is better than my way?...................6

2. Am I not a person? 6

3. Did you hear what South Carolina did?........................7

4. Who fired the first shot? 8

5. Why do they call him Stonewall?................................9

6. What are they doing in a cornfield? 10

7. Why are there two names?...11

8. What country does Lincoln lead now?........................12

9. Now who is in charge of the Northern army? 13

10. Just who is Jefferson Davis? 14

11. Who is that good-looking army officer? 15

12. Do we have to have peanut soup again? 16

13. Who said women cannnot help fight the war? 17

14. What will Lincoln do?..18

15. Did you hear that Lincoln said "forever free"? 18

16. Can we be soldiers now? 19

17. How did shoes start a battle?.....................................20

18. How shall we honor the soldiers? 21

19. How do you spell the name of that place? 22

20. What in the world does *E Pluribus Unum* mean? 22

Glossary 23

Index and Web Sites 24

The Civil War

Do you know what a civil war is? It is a war between two or more groups inside a country. Did you know that the United States had a civil war? It began in 1861 and lasted until 1865. People in the North and the South had different ways of life and different ideas about some subjects. These differences led to war. For a while, it was not certain whether the United States would remain one country or become two countries. However, those who wanted to keep the country together won the war. Keep reading to learn more about the Civil War.

This map shows the states that seceded, the states that stayed in the Union, and the Union states that allowed slavery.

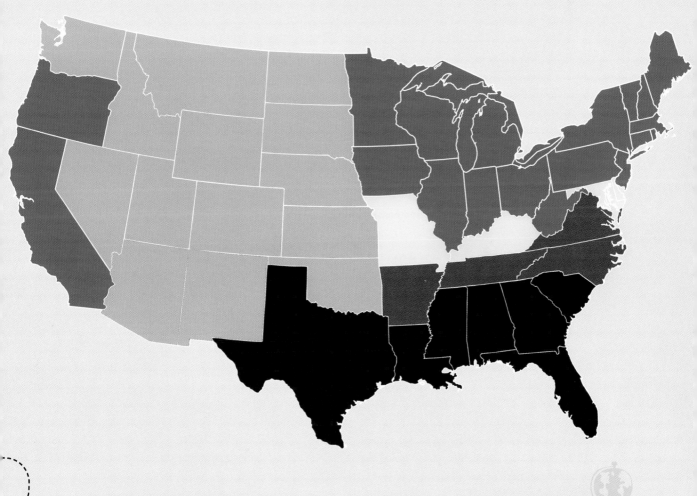

States that seceded before April 15, 1861
States that seceded after April 15, 1861
Union states that permitted slavery
Union states that banned slavery
Territories

1. Who said your way is better than my way?

Most Northerners lived in cities. Trade and factories formed the basis of the North's **economy**. Most Southerners lived in the countryside. The South's economy was based on farming. Southerners also believed each state had the right to run its government the way it wanted. The **federal** government could not tell states what to do.

2. Am I not a person?

The South's economy needed **slaves** to work on the large farms. Southerners thought of slaves as belongings. **Abolitionists** in the North believed slaves were people and slavery was wrong.

This is New York City in 1862. Northern cities were very different from Southern ones.

3. Did you hear what South Carolina did?

South Carolina **seceded** from the United States, in December 1860. Soon after, 10 more Southern states followed.

This is a Southern cotton plantation, or large farm. Plantation owners did not feel they could pay all the people they needed to run their farms.

Fort Sumter belonged to the Northern army. It was in the harbor of Charleston, South Carolina. The Southern army fired at the fort on April 12, 1861. The Civil War had begun.

Union soldiers are shown firing cannons, or large guns, during the Southern army's attack on Fort Sumter.

The first big land battle happened by a stream named Bull Run, in July 1861. This was near Manassas, Virginia. Northern **soldiers** charged Southern soldiers. A Southern officer named Thomas Jackson stood his ground as firmly as if he were a stone wall. He became known as Stonewall Jackson. Soon more Southern soldiers arrived. Northern soldiers ran away. The South had won the First Battle of Bull Run.

Stonewall Jackson was one of the best generals in the Southern army and in U.S. history. He was known for pushing his men to the limits and surprising the enemy.

9

6. What are they doing in a cornfield?

The South wanted to win a big battle in the North. Southerners thought it would help them get European aid. Thousands of Southern soldiers gathered on Antietam Creek, near Sharpsburg, Maryland. Northern and Southern soldiers fought in a cornfield for days. Finally, Southern soldiers withdrew. Northern soldiers said they won the Battle of Antietam.

The Battle of Antietam took place on September 17, 1862. It was the bloodiest single day of battle in American history.

The North and the South gave some battles different names. For example, the South called the First Battle of Bull Run the First Battle of Manassas. The North often named battles after nearby rivers or streams. The South commonly named the battles for towns or cities.

The Union spent part of the Battle of Antietam trying to win control of Antietam Creek's lower bridge. The bridge became known as Burnside's Bridge, after the Union leader who worked so hard to win the bridge.

Abraham Lincoln was voted president of the United States in 1860. The country was still called the United States even after the South seceded. It was also known as the Union. Lincoln remained president of the United States during the whole Civil War.

Lincoln was born, on February 12, 1809, in Kentucky. He believed strongly that it was his job to keep the Union together.

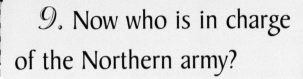

9. Now who is in charge of the Northern army?

As president, Lincoln picked the officer who would lead the Northern army. He tried many men before finding one he believed could win the war. That man was Ulysses S. Grant. Lincoln put Grant in command of the Northern army, in March 1864. Grant remained leader of the army until the North won the war, in 1865.

With General Ulysses S. Grant in command, the Union finally won the war. Grant later became the eighteenth president of the United States.

13

The Southern states formed their own country after they seceded. They called it the **Confederate States of America**. Southern leaders picked Jefferson Davis to be the country's president. He was president for the whole war.

Jefferson Davis had served as the U.S. secretary of war under President Franklin Pierce. He was also part of the U.S. Senate before he became the Confederate president.

Robert E. Lee is the man with the white beard in this picture. He did not agree with secession at first, but when his home state of Virginia seceded, he joined the Confederacy, too.

11. Who is that good-looking army officer?

Robert E. Lee was a good-looking man from a rich, famous Virginia family. He became a U.S. Army officer in 1829. He entered the Southern army after Virginia seceded, in 1861. Jefferson Davis made him commander of soldiers fighting in the East. Lee was an excellent soldier and leader. However, he did not have the men and supplies he needed to win the war.

12. Do we have to have peanut soup again?

A soldier's life was hard. Sometimes soldiers did not have enough clothes. Southern soldiers had bad shoes or no shoes at all. Soldiers might not have much food. Sometimes they made peanut soup from peanuts, water, and a little meat. Sickness was a problem. More soldiers died from sickness than from being hurt in battle. For fun, soldiers wrote letters, played games, and sang.

These Confederate soldiers are playing cards to pass the time.

Clara Barton is well known for her work during the Civil War. She also went on to found the Red Cross.

The Northern and Southern armies did not allow women. However, some women dressed as men to become soldiers. Other women helped by **spying** on the enemy. Others helped by nursing soldiers who were hurt or sick.

Here nurses are shown taking care of Union soldiers at this field hospital.

14. What will Lincoln do?

Lincoln believed slavery was wrong. He decided to take action to end it. He sent out a statement five days after the Battle of Antietam. He said he would free the South's slaves if the South did not quit fighting.

15. Did you hear that Lincoln said "forever free"?

The South refused to quit fighting. On January 1, 1863, Lincoln sent out the **Emancipation Proclamation**. It said slaves in the states fighting against the North were "forever free."

Here President Lincoln reads the Emancipation Proclamation to his advisers.

16. Can we be soldiers now?

The Emancipation Proclamation also said African Americans could become Northern soldiers. Thousands did. About 200,000 African Americans fought in the Civil War. About 35,000 of them died.

By the President of the United States of America:

A Proclamation.

Whereas, on the twenty-second day of September, in the year of our Lord one thousand eight hundred and sixty-two, a proclamation was issued by the President of the United States, containing, among other things, the following, to wit:

"That on the first day of January, in the year of our Lord one thousand eight hundred and sixty-three, all persons held as slaves within any State or designated part of a State, the people whereof shall then be in rebellion against the United States, shall be then, thenceforward, and forever free; and the Executive Government of the United States, including the military and naval authority thereof, will recognize and maintain the freedom of such persons, and will do no act

Here two African-American Union soldiers aim with their guns ready to fire.

19

17. How did shoes start a battle?

Southern soldiers were looking for shoes when they ran into Northern soldiers near Gettysburg, Pennsylvania, on July 1, 1863. Fighting began. The Battle of Gettysburg lasted three days. About 23,000 Northern soldiers were dead or hurt when it ended. About 25,000 Southern soldiers were dead or hurt. The Southern army never again became strong.

The Battle of Gettysburg lasted for three days. It was a turning point in the war.

Northern leaders gathered at Gettysburg in November 1863 to honor the soldiers who died there. Lincoln gave a famous speech called the Gettysburg Address. He said the North must win the war to guard "government of the people, by the people, and for the people."

Lincoln used the Gettysburg Address to remind everyone what they were fighting for and why the Union was so important. The speech lasted only about two minutes.

21

19. How do you spell the name of that place?

The North and South fought hard battles in 1864 and 1865. Then Northern soldiers trapped Southern soldiers at a small Virginia settlement called Appomattox Courthouse. Lee knew it was time to give up. He **surrendered** to Grant there, on April 9, 1865. The war was over.

20. What in the world does *E Pluribus Unum* mean?

E Pluribus Unum is the motto, or saying, of the United States. It is Latin for "out of many, one." It means one country was formed out of 13 different **colonies**. People were not sure the nation could remain one country when the Civil War began. However, the nation did. The motto was a good one.

22

Glossary

abolitionists (a-buh-LIH-shun-ists) People who worked to end slavery.

colonies (KAH-luh-neez) New places where people move that are still ruled by the leaders of the country from which they came.

Confederate States of America (kun-FEH-duh-ret STAYTS UV uh-MER-ih-kuh) A group of 11 Southern states that announced themselves free from the United States in 1860 and 1861.

economy (ih-KAH-nuh-mee) The way in which a country or a business oversees its goods and services.

Emancipation Proclamation (ih-man-sih-PAY-shun pro-kluh-MAY-shun) A paper, signed by Abraham Lincoln during the Civil War, that freed all slaves held in Southern land.

federal (FEH-duh-rul) Having to do with the central government.

seceded (sih-SEED-ed) Withdrew from a group or a country.

slaves (SLAYVZ) People who are "owned" by another person and forced to work for him or her.

soldiers (SOHL-jurz) People who are in an army.

spying (SPY-ing) Watching secretly.

surrendered (suh-REN-derd) Gave up.

Index

A
Appomattox
Courthouse, 22

B
Battle of Antietam,
10, 18

C
Confederate States
of America, 14

D
Davis, Jefferson, 14,
15

E
Emancipation
Proclamation, 18,
19

F
Fort Sumter, 8

L
Lee, Robert E., 15,
22
Lincoln, Abraham,
12, 13, 18, 21

S
slave(s), 6, 18

U
Union, 12

Web Sites

Due to the changing nature of Internet links, PowerKids Press has developed an online list of Web sites related to the subject of this book. This site is updated regularly. Please use this link to access the list:
www.powerkidslinks.com/20his/ciwar/